TUNDRA
ECOSYSTEMS

by Cecilia Pinto McCarthy

12 STORY LIBRARY

www.12StoryLibrary.com

12-Story Library is an imprint of Bookstaves and Press Room Editions

Produced for 12-Story Library by Red Line Editorial

Photographs ©: Nordroden/Shutterstock Images, cover, 1; Incredible Arctic/Shutterstock Images, 4; Gregory A. Pozhvanov/Shutterstock Images, 5, 24; mapichai/iStockphoto, 6; Vladimir Melnik/ Shutterstock Images, 7, 21; Bildagentur Zoonar GmbH/Shutterstock Images, 8; NancyS/Shutterstock Images, 9; outdoorsman/Shutterstock Images, 10, 28 (top left); Dennis W Donohue/Shutterstock Images, 11, 28 (top right); nate samui/Shutterstock Images, 12; Rasmus Holmboe Dahl/Shutterstock Images, 13; Wolfgang Kruck/Shutterstock Images, 14; John Wijsman/Shutterstock Images, 15; Vadim Nefedoff/Shutterstock Images, 16–17; Valentina Photo/Shutterstock Images, 17; Marzolino/ Shutterstock Images, 18; Andrea Izzotti/Shutterstock Images, 19; Kai Mortensen/Shutterstock Images, 20; V. Belov/Shutterstock Images, 22; vchal/Shutterstock Images, 23; Jan Martin Will/Shutterstock Images, 25; I. Noyan Yilmaz/Shutterstock Images, 26; BMJ/Shutterstock Images, 27; Grigorii Pisotsckii/ Shutterstock Images, 28 (bottom); Erni/Shutterstock Images, 29 (top left); Karelian/Shutterstock Images, 29 (top right); robas/iStockphoto, 29 (middle); Sergey Krasnoshchokov/Shutterstock Images, 29 (bottom)

Content Consultant: Jeffery Welker, Professor of Biological Sciences, University of Alaska Anchorage

Library of Congress Cataloging-in-Publication Data
Names: McCarthy, Cecilia Pinto.
Title: Tundra ecosystems / by Cecilia Pinto McCarthy.
Description: Mankato, MN : 12 Story Library, [2018] | Series: Earth's
  ecosystems | Audience: Grade 4 to 6. | Includes bibliographical references
  and index.
Identifiers: LCCN 2016047135 (print) | LCCN 2016047752 (ebook) | ISBN
  9781632354594 (hardcover : alk. paper) | ISBN 9781632355256 (pbk. : alk.
  paper) | ISBN 9781621435778 (hosted e-book)
Subjects: LCSH: Tundra ecology--Juvenile literature.
Classification: LCC QH541.5.T8 M44 2018 (print) | LCC QH541.5.T8 (ebook) |
  DDC 577.5/86--dc23
LC record available at https://lccn.loc.gov/2016047135

Printed in China
022017

Access free, up-to-date content on this topic plus a full digital version of this book. Scan the QR code on page 31 or use your school's login at 12StoryLibrary.com.

Table of Contents

The Tundra Is an Extreme Biome

Near the Arctic Circle lies a vast area blanketed by snow for most of the year. Here, winter temperatures average a bone-chilling minus 30 degrees Fahrenheit (−34°C). Frosty winds whip at 30 to 60 miles per hour (48 to 97 km/h). This frigid land is the Arctic tundra.

The tundra is one of Earth's many biomes. Biomes are grouped by their climate. Each one is home to certain types of plants and animals. The tundra is the world's coldest biome. Beneath the surface lies permanently frozen ground called permafrost. Only the top layer of thin soil thaws on warmer days in the summer.

The average temperature in the Arctic tundra is 10 to 20 degrees Fahrenheit (−12 to −6.7°C).

In some tundra areas, permafrost formed 10,000 to 20,000 years ago.

In certain places, the tundra can be one of the driest parts of Earth. It is considered a cold desert. It gets less than 10 inches (25 cm) of precipitation a year. Most comes as snow, but there are some rain showers in the summer.

There are three types of tundra: Arctic, Antarctic, and Alpine. Arctic tundra is found north of the Arctic Circle, on the land that surrounds the Arctic Ocean. Antarctic tundra covers parts of the Antarctic Peninsula and West Antarctica. Alpine tundra is found above the tree line in the mountains of places with temperate climates.

50
Degrees, in Fahrenheit (10°C), of the warmest summer temperatures in the tundra.

- The tundra is the world's coldest biome.
- Tundra biomes are found in the Arctic, the Antarctic Peninsula, West Antarctica, and above the tree line in certain places.
- Permafrost is permanently frozen ground found in the tundra.

THINK ABOUT IT

Write a short description of the climate where you live. What are the seasons like? Is it ever very cold or very hot? Use the Internet to find the average yearly temperatures where you live.

The Tundra Has Only Two Seasons

Seasons are caused by the tilt of Earth on its axis. Depending on the time of year, different parts of the planet get more direct sunlight. When the northern hemisphere is tilted toward the sun, it is summer in the Arctic and winter in the Antarctic. The seasons reverse six months later, when the northern hemisphere is tilted away from the sun.

During the winter months in the tundra, the days are dark and cold. The sun rises only slightly above the horizon. On the winter solstice, the sun does not rise at all in parts of the Arctic and the Antarctic. Temperatures stay well below freezing.

The amount of sun different parts of Earth receives depends on the tilt of Earth on its axis.

Seasons in the Northern Hemisphere

Spring

Winter

Summer

Autumn

Direction of orbit

PINGOS

The yearly freezing and thawing of tundra ground creates land formations called pingos. These cone-shaped mounds form when small pools of water collect underground. The water becomes trapped by permafrost. The freeze-thaw cycle pushes the ground upward. The world's tallest pingo is Ibyuk, found on Canada's Tuktoyaktuk Peninsula. It is about 160 feet (49 m) high.

2
Number of months plants are able to grow in the tundra.

- Seasons happen because Earth tilts on its axis as it travels around the sun.
- During the tundra winter, the sun rises only slightly above the horizon or not all.
- The sun shines 24 hours a day in the summer, but temperatures stay cool.
- Melting permafrost provides water for plants to grow.

During summer in the Arctic, the sun shines high in the sky and never sets. Despite the sunlight, temperatures remain fairly cool. Some of the ice and snow melt. Below the surface, the meltwater cannot soak into the permafrost. Water pools on the ground, forming soggy bogs and marshy ponds. Seeds sprout and plants begin to grow. After a long winter, the tundra comes alive.

Tundra plants take advantage of summer's 24 hours of sunlight and grow quickly before winter arrives.

Permafrost Limits Plant Growth

Plants need sunlight, nutrients, and water to grow. In the tundra, these elements can be scarce. The soil has limited nutrients, and water is often frozen. But tundra plants have adapted to survive. Some parts of the tundra have 24 hours of sunlight in summer. This means plants can grow all day long during the growing season, which lasts 50 to 60 days.

Few trees and tall plants grow on the tundra. In places where there is deep snow, tall shrubs can survive. The snow protects their buds from icy winds. Most tundra plants are small and low to the ground. Short plants, such as cushion plants, form tight masses that trap heat. They spread like a green carpet across rocky tundra soil.

Tundra plants, such as dwarf willow shrubs, thrive in the tundra.

Some plants have special stems and leaves. They hold in heat and water. Some flowers turn and follow the sun as it moves across the sky.

Adaptations such as thick, hairy stems and leaves help tundra plants thrive.

Places where birds nest and arctic foxes make dens have rich soil. In these areas, bird droppings, fox scat, and food scraps decompose. The rotted material enriches the soil. In the summer, the nesting and denning spots come alive with lush flowering gardens.

LIVELY LICHENS

Lichens grow in both the Arctic and Alpine tundra. They grow in crusty or leafy patches on rocks and soil. A lichen is not a plant. It is part fungus and part algae. Using the sun's energy, the algae makes food for itself and the fungus. The fungus adds water and minerals it absorbs from its surroundings. Lichens are some of the only foods available for caribou and musk ox in winter.

1,700
Types of plants that grow in the Arctic tundra.

- Plants need sunlight, water, and soil to grow.
- Tundra plants have adaptations that allow them to survive in poor growing conditions.
- Small plants with shallow roots do well in the tundra.

9

Animals Need Adaptations to Survive

Most tundra animals are mammals and birds. Predators, such as arctic foxes and polar bears, prowl the icy land and sea. Their prey includes seals, lemmings, hares, and caribou. Birds such as gyrfalcons, arctic terns, and snowy owls hunt from the sky. On the ground, rock ptarmigans eat plant buds, insects, and berries.

Mammals and birds need to keep their bodies warm. They prepare for winter by eating large amounts of food. A thick layer of fat builds up under their skin. The fat gives them the energy and warmth they need to survive the winter. Other animals, such as arctic ground squirrels, hibernate in winter. They dig dens into the tundra and awaken from time to time.

Many mammals grow extra fur for protection. Musk ox grow a thick undercoat against their skin.

A polar bear's fat keeps it warm in icy waters.

THE SUBNIVEAN LAYER

Small mammals, such voles and lemmings, need deep snow to survive the winter. They live in the subnivean layer. This is an area above the ground but beneath the snowpack. The deep snow acts like a blanket. Heat rising from the ground becomes trapped under the snow. The temperature in the subnivean layer is higher than the temperature above the snow.

Long, coarse hairs on top of the undercoat keep the musk ox dry. Caribou and polar bears have hollow hairs filled with air. The air insulates them against the cold. Some birds, such as snowy owls and ptarmigans, grow extra layers of feathers. Feathers trap warmth and repel water. Fur and feathers also provide camouflage. During the summer, some animals are dark in color. As winter approaches, they turn white.

100

Pounds (45 kg) of seal blubber a polar bear can eat in one sitting.

- Mammals and birds make up the greatest population of Arctic tundra animals.
- Artic animals include arctic foxes, polar bears, snowy owls, lemmings, and caribou.
- Animal adaptations include extra body fat, thicker fur, hollow hairs, added feathers, and hibernation.

A musk ox sheds its thick undercoat in spring each year.

Millions of Mosquitoes Swarm in Summer

In the summer months, millions of mosquitoes swarm the Arctic tundra. In July and August, mosquitoes lay their eggs in or near water. Early the following year, mosquitoes emerge from the water all at once. They form huge swarms that bite and pester tundra animals. Mosquitoes disturb feeding and breeding caribou. Caribou often flee to colder, windier areas to avoid mosquitoes.

Like mosquitoes, other insects and invertebrates have adapted to the harsh tundra climate. Examples include flies, beetles, springtails, spiders, and arctic bumblebees. Despite their tiny size, they can survive the cold, dry climate. Many insects live on the ground or in the top layer of soil. Others take shelter in crevices or plants. These areas tend to be warm and moist.

Insects that cannot tolerate cold weather produce a special protein in their bodies. The protein

Mosquitoes are common in the Arctic tundra.

SOMETHING TO SNEEZE ABOUT

During the summer, caribou sometimes look as if they are dancing. They shake their heads and stamp their feet. They are trying to keep botflies away. Female botflies lay maggots in or near a caribou's nostrils. The maggots make their way into the animal's nose and into its throat. Months later, the maggots detach themselves. The caribou cough or sneeze the maggots into the soil. The maggots become adult flies, and the cycle continues.

acts like antifreeze. It lowers the freezing point of water in the insects' bodies. It stops ice crystals from forming inside the insect.

Some insects, such as arctic bumblebees, have dark, hairy bodies. The dark color absorbs what little heat is available. Hairs trap heat against the insects' fragile bodies.

2,200
Number of insect species that live in the Arctic tundra.

- Mosquitoes swarm by the millions during the summer.
- Insects survive by living in the soil, in rock cracks, or on plants.
- Some insects have a protein that acts like antifreeze in their bodies.
- Some insects have dark, hairy bodies that absorb and hold heat.

The Jutta Arctic is a type of butterfly that lives in tundra regions.

Birds Migrate to the Tundra

The Arctic tundra is an important breeding and feeding ground for migratory birds. Birds take advantage of the vast food supply in summer to mate and raise their young. Before winter returns, they leave for warmer regions.

Red-necked phalaropes nest in the Arctic tundra.

44,000

Distance, in miles (70,811 km), an arctic tern migrates to and from the Arctic tundra each year.

- Millions of birds migrate to the Arctic tundra every year.
- They come to nest, lay eggs, and raise their young.
- The tundra provides the food and nesting space the birds need.
- Some birds use their time in the tundra to molt before flying to their winter homes.

The Lapland longspur is also known as the Lapland bunting.

Every year, millions of birds arrive in the Arctic tundra from all over the world. Insects, fish, and berries provide nutrition for adult birds and their young. Shorebirds, ducks, geese, songbirds, and swans stake out places to build their nests. Red-necked phalaropes and dunlins choose marshy areas around ponds and lakes. Lapland longspurs tuck their grass nests into mossy dips in the ground. By mid-July, most eggs have hatched. Chicks must grow fast and fledge before the cold weather sets in.

Many waterfowl use their time in the tundra to molt. Their old, worn feathers fall out. New feathers grow in their place. The process can take several weeks. Molting birds are easy targets for predators, such as the arctic fox. To keep safe, the birds stay in areas where there is plenty of food and shelter. They put on extra fat for their return trip south.

Arctic Peoples Blend Different Ways of Life

People have lived in the Arctic tundra for thousands of years. Indigenous peoples believe they have always lived in the Arctic. Scientists believe the first group of early people traveled from Siberia through what is now Alaska at least 15,000 years ago.

Early Arctic peoples were nomadic and lived in small family groups. They hunted fish, walrus, whales, seals, and caribou. These animals provided meat for food and skins that were sewn to make clothes. Bones and stones were carved into tools. People lived off the land, harvesting berries, herbs, and other plants.

Kangamiut is an Arctic village in Greenland.

Indigenous peoples make up about 10 percent of the Arctic population. They include

SAMI REINDEER HERDERS

The Sami people of Scandinavia and Russia are reindeer herders. They use reindeer for meat, fur, and transportation. At one time, Sami herders followed their herds as they migrated hundreds of miles. Now, modern Sami herders have land where they keep their reindeer.

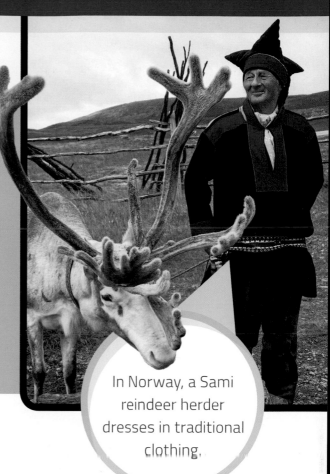

In Norway, a Sami reindeer herder dresses in traditional clothing.

the Inuit, Yup'ik, Sami, Chukchi, and Nenet. They live in the United States, Greenland, Canada, Norway, and Finland. They also live in Sweden, Iceland, Denmark, and Russia. Each group has its own traditions, culture, and language. Modern Arctic peoples combine traditional and new ways of life.

40

Approximate number of different ethnic groups living in the Arctic.

- Early Arctic peoples lived off the land.
- They were nomadic and followed migrating animals, such as caribou.
- Today, Arctic peoples follow both traditional and modern ways of life.

17

Early Explorers Faced Challenges

For a long time, ice, snow, and extreme cold kept explorers away from the Arctic. But European explorers wanted a shorter trade route to Asia. They hoped to find a Northwest Passage through Arctic waters.

Starting in the 1700s, European, Russian, and US sailors and explorers began arriving in the Arctic. They overhunted whales, walrus, and musk ox. Arctic peoples relied on these animals for survival. Explorers spread deadly diseases, such as

In 1845, Sir John Franklin sailed into the Canadian Arctic in search of the Northwest Passage.

smallpox, that killed thousands of Arctic peoples. They introduced new ways of life that interfered with the culture and traditions of Arctic peoples.

Ship crews brought liquor into villages. Arctic peoples began to suffer from social problems, such as addiction and violence. When missionaries arrived, they brought new religions and built schools. Arctic family life changed, and Arctic peoples stopped being nomadic.

Explorers and their crews faced life-threatening hazards. Many voyages ended when ships became trapped by sea ice. Crews battled disease, hunger, and extreme cold. Finally, Norwegian explorer Roald Amundsen successfully sailed through the Northwest Passage in 1906.

1903

Year Roald Amundsen began his Arctic exploration.

- The Arctic's extreme conditions made exploration difficult.
- Early Arctic explorers fought against bitter cold, ice, snow, and disease.
- Norwegian explorer Roald Amundsen made the first successful voyage through the Northwest Passage.

A statue of Roald Amundsen can be found in Tromso, Norway.

Humans Damage the Fragile Tundra Biome

The tundra is rich in natural resources, such as oil, natural gas, and minerals. People drill and mine these resources. This can harm the tundra biome. Companies dig and build pipelines to get at oil and gas underground. The process involves large machines and vehicles. They damage lichens and plants. It takes years for slow-growing vegetation to grow back.

Even more damage happens when workers and their families move to job sites. Construction of buildings uses land needed by plants and animals. Habitats are split into smaller areas when roads are put in. This disrupts migration routes for animals, such as caribou. They must find new ways to get around the places where people have moved in.

A coal mine in Longyearbyen, Norway

Offshore drilling makes problems for marine creatures. Pollution in the air and water harms marine animals. Oil spills damage land and water. They kill plants and animals. In Siberia, industries cause air and chemical pollution. When people visit Arctic areas, they bring trash. Plastic bags, fishing equipment, and old fuel tanks can be found even in the most remote places.

Pollution can cause problems for Arctic plants and animals.

ARCTIC ANIMAL EXTINCTIONS

One of the tundra's most important resources is its wildlife. Animals are a source of food, oil, and other materials. Hunters and whalers first came to the Arctic to harvest wildlife. Overhunting greatly reduced populations of some animals and birds. The slow-moving Steller's sea cow was easy to catch. By 1768, sea cows were extinct. The great auk is a type of flightless bird. It was hunted for its meat, feathers, and fat. The great auk has been extinct since 1844.

13
Percentage of the world's undiscovered oil estimated to be in the Arctic.

- The tundra contains important natural resources, such as oil, natural gas, and minerals.
- Extracting natural resources damages the tundra and its plants and animals.
- Humans have brought plastic bags, discarded equipment, and other types of pollution with them to the tundra.

21

Melting Permafrost Releases Carbon

When people use cars and electricity or run factories, they burn fuels, such as oil, gas, and coal. This releases extra greenhouse gases into the atmosphere. The excess gases trap heat. This makes Earth warmer. The warmer climate is changing Arctic weather patterns, melting glaciers and sea ice, and raising sea levels.

The tundra is a carbon sink, or a place that stores carbon. The permafrost contains organic matter. It is made up of dead plants and animals that have been frozen for thousands of years. But climate change is thawing permafrost. As it thaws, the organic matter rots. Bacteria eat the rotting matter and give off carbon dioxide and

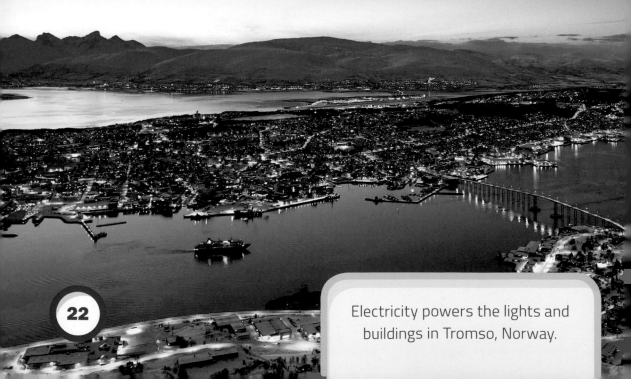

Electricity powers the lights and buildings in Tromso, Norway.

methane gas. Instead of trapping carbon, the tundra is releasing greenhouse gases into the atmosphere.

Thawing permafrost uncovers other hidden dangers. Thawing animal carcasses contain anthrax and other deadly bacteria. Frozen anthrax can stay alive for more than 100 years. In 2016, a caribou carcass in Siberia thawed. Anthrax spread, killing more than 2,000 reindeer and one person. Many other people became seriously ill.

Percentage of the world's soil carbon that is stored in Arctic permafrost.

- Greenhouse gases trap heat in the atmosphere around Earth.
- Tundra permafrost acts as a carbon sink.
- Thawing permafrost releases greenhouse gases, dangerous bacteria, and viruses into the environment.

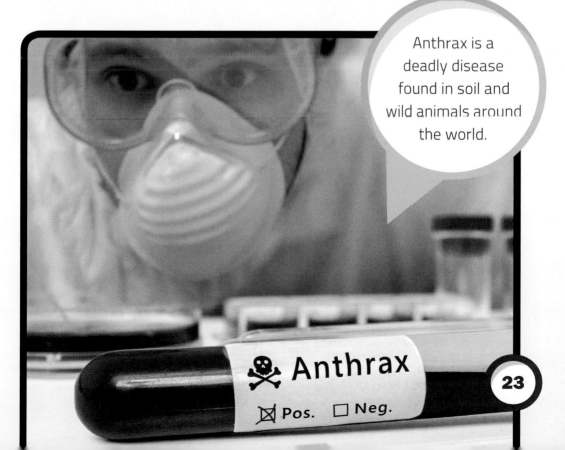

Anthrax is a deadly disease found in soil and wild animals around the world.

☠ Anthrax

☒ Pos.   ☐ Neg.

Climate Change Threatens the Tundra

Climate change is threatening the tundra ecosystem. Scientists have seen that temperatures are increasing faster in the Arctic and the Antarctic than anywhere else in the world.

Climate change is making the Arctic tundra a greener place. Under normal conditions, only small, low-growing plants can survive the tundra's harsh weather. As the tundra warms, shrubs and other plants are growing larger than normal. One day, the Arctic may be warm enough for even tall trees to grow.

Willow bushes and dwarf birch grow in the Russian tundra.

Polar bears stand on sea ice to hunt their prey, but there is less ice due to climate change.

Wildlife is also affected by increasing temperatures. Warmer temperatures are melting sea ice. Sea ice is important to Arctic animals. Without ice to stand on, polar bears cannot catch seals. They must travel great distances in search of food. Some starve to death.

THINK ABOUT IT

How do you think climate change will affect you and the people you know?

1.5

Degrees, in Fahrenheit (0.8°C), of the average temperature increase over the past 100 years across the globe.

- Temperatures are increasing on the tundra faster than anywhere else on the planet.
- Warming temperatures allow larger plants to grow on the tundra.
- When sea ice melts, polar bears cannot hunt seals.

People Work Together to Save the Tundra

The tundra is one of the world's most important biomes. What happens in the tundra shapes events on the entire planet. Saving the tundra is a difficult task. It takes the cooperation and action of people worldwide. Scientists, citizens, and organizations are working together to make a difference.

Scientists are looking for new methods and technologies that capture or reduce greenhouse gases. Special equipment captures and stores the gases. Another way to reduce greenhouse gases is to use clean energy sources. Clean energy sources, such as wind and solar power, do not burn fuels. Other new concepts include energy-efficient buildings and cars that use less energy.

Conservation groups research ways to save tundra plants and animals. They work to limit human activities

Scientists have set up research stations in Antarctica.

Scientists examine an Arctic fox in Sweden.

that destroy tundra habitat, such as mining and construction.

Each day, people can do their part to protect tundra ecosystems. They can bike rather than drive. They can turn off appliances when not in use. They can reduce waste and recycle. Together, people must find ways to reduce climate change or risk losing the fragile tundra.

THINK ABOUT IT

Make a list of things you do that can help slow climate change. What other things can you add to your list?

37

Percentage of carbon dioxide emissions that come from generating electricity in the United States.

- Scientists are developing new technologies and ways of reducing greenhouse gases.
- Wind and solar power are examples of clean energy sources.
- People can help slow climate change by conserving energy, recycling, and reducing waste.

Tundra Food Web

musk ox

polar bear

lichen

28

lemming

arctic fox

cushion plant

caribou

Glossary

adapted
Changed to fit a situation.

biomes
Communities of plants and animals.

camouflage
A protective coloration in animals that helps them blend in with their environments.

climate
The weather in a particular place.

decompose
To rot.

fledge
To grow feathers for flying.

frigid
Very cold.

hemisphere
One half of Earth; usually northern and southern or eastern and western.

invertebrates
Creatures without a backbone.

nomadic
A way of life in which people move from place to place.

precipitation
Water that falls to the ground as snow or rain.

protein
A molecule that is an important part of living cells.

scat
Animal waste.

For More Information

Books

Benoit, Peter. *Tundra*. New York: Children's Press, 2011.

Gagne, Tammy. *Tundra Ecosystems*. Minneapolis, MN: Abdo Publishing, 2015.

Woodford, Chris. *Arctic Tundra and Polar Deserts*. Chicago: Heinemann-Raintree, 2011.

Visit 12StoryLibrary.com

Scan the code or use your school's login at **12StoryLibrary.com** for recent updates about this topic and a full digital version of this book. Enjoy free access to:

- Digital ebook
- Breaking news updates
- Live content feeds
- Videos, interactive maps, and graphics
- Additional web resources

Note to educators: Visit 12StoryLibrary.com/register to sign up for free premium website access. Enjoy live content plus a full digital version of every 12-Story Library book you own for every student at your school.

Index

About the Author

Cecilia Pinto McCarthy has written several nonfiction books for children. She also teaches environmental science classes at a nature sanctuary. She lives with her family north of Boston, Massachusetts.

READ MORE FROM 12-STORY LIBRARY

Every 12-Story Library book is available in many formats. For more information, visit 12StoryLibrary.com.